The Great Depression

CORNERSTONES OF FREEDOM™

SECOND SERIES

Elaine Landau

Children's Press
An Imprint of Scholastic Inc.
New York • Toronto • London • Auckland • Sydney
Mexico City • New Delhi • Hong Kong
Danbury, Connecticut

Photographs © 2007: AP/Wide World Photos: 4, 22, 29; Brown Brothers: 10, 11, 25; Corbis Images: 3, 6, 8, 21, 27 (Bettmann), 12 (John Vachon); Franklin D. Roosevelt Library: cover top, 14, 33; Getty Images/Hulton Archive: 20, 30 (American Stock), 31 (Keystone), 24; Library of Congress: cover bottom (Dorothea Lange), 7, 15, 16, 35, 36, 39, 40; PhotoEdit/Myrleen Ferguson Cate: 41; Stock Montage, Inc.: 28; Underwood & Underwood: 18, 19.

Map by XNR Productions, Inc.

Library of Congress Cataloging-in-Publication Data
Landau, Elaine.
  The Great Depression / Elaine Landau.
     p. cm. — (Cornerstones of Freedom. Second series)
  Includes bibliographical references and index.

  ISBN-13: 978-0-516-23622-3 (lib. bdg.)   978-0-531-18767-8 (pbk.)

  ISBN-10: 0-516-23622-9 (lib. bdg.)   0-531-18767-5 (pbk.)

 1. New Deal, 1933–1939—Juvenile literature. 2. Depressions—1929—United States—Juvenile literature. 3. United States—Economic conditions—1918–1945—Juvenile literature. 4. United States—Social conditions—1933–1945—Juvenile literature. 5. United States—History—1933–1945—Juvenile literature. I. Title. II. Series.
  E806.L28 2006   2005007526

5 6 7 8 9 10 R 17 16 15 14 13 12 11   62

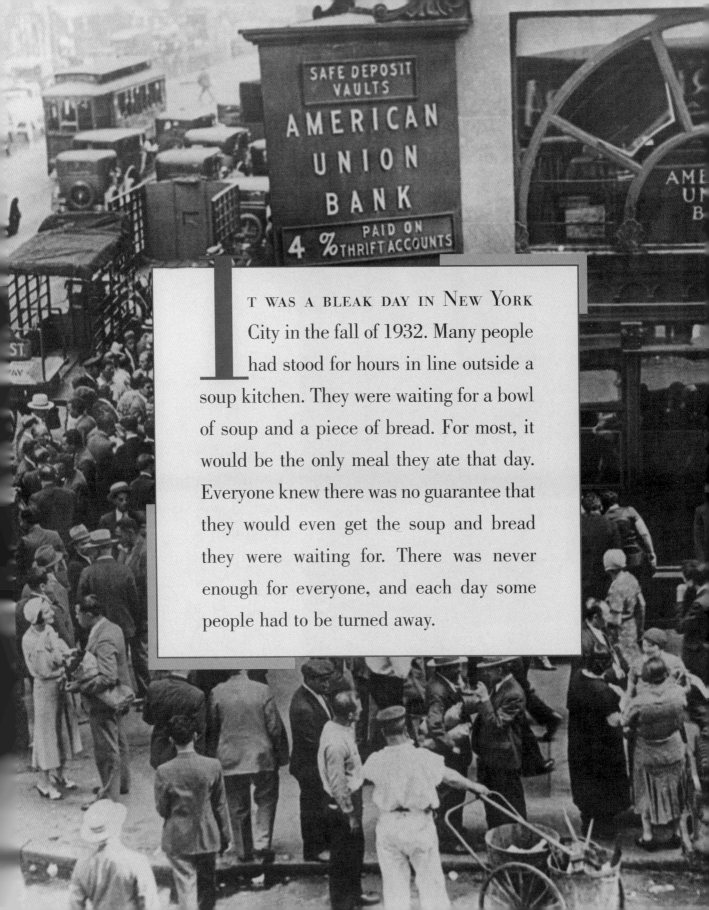

I T WAS A BLEAK DAY IN NEW YORK City in the fall of 1932. Many people had stood for hours in line outside a soup kitchen. They were waiting for a bowl of soup and a piece of bread. For most, it would be the only meal they ate that day. Everyone knew there was no guarantee that they would even get the soup and bread they were waiting for. There was never enough for everyone, and each day some people had to be turned away.

SAFE DEPOSIT VAULTS
AMERICAN UNION BANK
4 % PAID ON THRIFT ACCOUNTS

Without any means of support, families across the nation were forced to stand in line for hours on end in the hopes of receiving much-needed food.

Meanwhile, in another part of the city, hundreds of others, including children, gathered near the river. They were waiting for the city's garbage trucks to arrive at the dump. After the trucks dumped out their loads of garbage, those waiting would rush over to **scavenge** for anything they could eat.

Life had not always been this way, but hard times had hit the nation. In New York City, as well as in other parts of the country, people were out of work. They had lived on their savings for a while, but now all their money was gone. Some of these people were immigrants who had come to America seeking a better life. But their American dream had turned into a nightmare. Their enthusiasm and hope for the future had been replaced by despair. America was struggling through the longest and most severe financial downturn in its history (to that time). The period known as the Great Depression began in 1929 and lasted until the early 1940s.

HOW IT HAPPENED

Most people trace the start of the Great Depression to October 29, 1929—the day known as Black Tuesday. That was the day the **stock market** crashed, crushing the hopes, dreams, and financial well-being of many Americans. The stock market crash had a devastating effect on the **economy**. That was because many people who had hoped to get rich quickly had bought their **stock** on margin. This means they paid from 10 percent to 50 percent of the stock's price up front and borrowed the rest of the money to pay for it. This was fine as long as the price of the stock went up. However, when the price of stocks dropped, people had to pay back the money they had borrowed. When the price of stocks dropped rapidly between October 24 and October 29, people were unable to pay back their loans. This caused the banks they borrowed from to fail. Many businesses lost their credit lines and had to close.

Other factors played a role in this terrible economic period. Among them was what many perceived as the imbalance of wealth in the United States. A line from a popular song during the 1920s is "the rich get richer and the poor get poorer," and in some ways that is exactly what happened. During the 1920s, the profits of large companies skyrocketed, but salaries for most working-class Americans largely remained the same. In 1929, the wealthiest Americans—

SAVING THE CENTRAL PARK SHEEP

A large, beautiful park was created in the heart of New York City in the mid-1800s. Known as Central Park, it was enjoyed by New Yorkers and visitors alike. To make visiting the park feel like being in the country, a herd of sheep was brought in. They grazed in an area of the park called Sheep Meadow, and people enjoyed watching them.

During the Great Depression, many people in the city were hungry and desperate. The sheep were thought to be at risk. Officials feared that the animals might be stolen and used for food. For the herd's protection, the animals were taken to a farm in upstate New York. The sheep stayed there safely for the remainder of their lives.

George Eastman, founder of the Eastman Kodak Company. Eastman's company, like so many others, made large profits, but employee salaries remained the same.

only about 1 million of the nation's total population of 123 million—had about 40 percent of the country's wealth. The other 60 percent of the wealth was divided among the remaining 122 million people.

At the same time, more than half of all Americans barely had enough money to make ends meet. Many were too poor to make a lot of purchases. With few people buying their **goods**, factories soon closed, putting large numbers of people out of work. This left even fewer people with money to purchase products. As a result, increasing numbers of businesses failed, and hard times continued to spread throughout the nation.

The crisis worsened as numerous American farms failed. Like businesses, farms were producing more food than people could afford to buy. During the Great Depression, this drove prices down to about half of what they had been. The farmers could not make enough money to survive.

Still another factor in the Great Depression was the many bank failures throughout the country. After World War I (1914–1918), large American banks had loaned money to European nations so that those countries could repay their war debts. But as poor economic times spread internationally, many European countries

A DAY LIKE NO OTHER

A guard at the New York **Stock Exchange** described what it was like on the **trading floor** on October 29, 1929:

"They [**stockbrokers** and investors] roared like a lot of lions and tigers. They hollered and screamed. . . . It was like a bunch of crazy men. Every once in a while when [large companies that traded many stocks] would take another [price drop], you'd see some poor devil collapse and fall to the floor."

There were often reports of some **tycoons** on **Wall Street** jumping to their deaths from high-rise buildings. They could not face the despair of having lost all their money in only one day.

An abandoned farm in Madison County, Montana

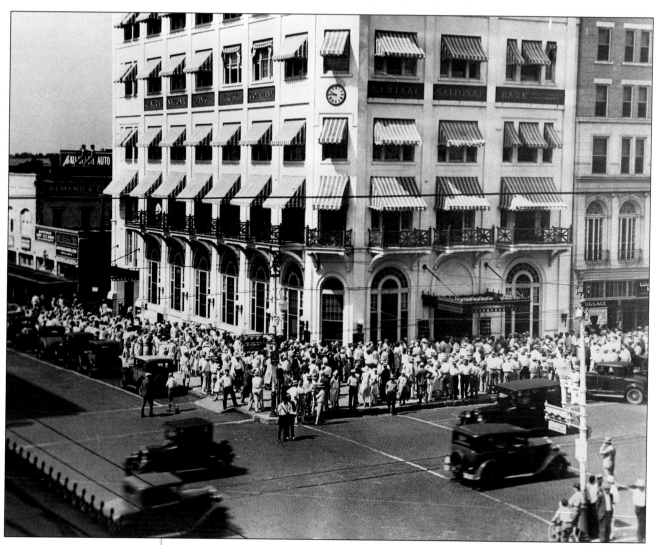

As banks began to close in financial ruin, panicked crowds of people rushed to withdraw their savings before it disappeared.

were unable to pay back the money. Things worsened for the banks, as large numbers of U.S. farms and businesses were also unable to meet their loan payments. These conditions forced many banks to close their doors. People saw the closings and panicked. They rushed to the banks that were still open and withdrew all their money, causing even more banks to shut their doors because they had no money left.

Things went from bad to worse in the summer of 1931, when an eight-year severe **drought** hit the southern portion of the Great Plains. This fertile farm region is where many of the country's major crops are grown. During the drought, however, dust storms ripped across the area, covering it with a thick blanket of sand and dust. Life for the farm families in this region was drastically changed. The windswept dust made taking a walk, riding a bike, and even breathing quite difficult. Doors and windows were kept shut at all times, even in the hottest weather, but the dust still found its way inside people's homes. Farmers could not grow crops in the dry dusty soil. The region quickly became known as the Dust Bowl.

SCRAPING BY AND RIDING THE RAILS

Jobs were few and far between during the Great Depression. The few jobs that became available often resulted in responses from thousands of people in need of work. By about 1933, unemployment in the United States reached its highest level. Nearly 16 million people, or about one-fourth of the country's workforce, were out of work.

Working people on all levels were severely affected. Many doctors, architects, engineers, and other professionals were unable to make a living at what they were trained to do, because their patients or clients could no longer afford to pay them. In New York City, some people—no

THEY RODE THE RAILS

Some of the men who rode the rails during the Great Depression later became famous. Among them were:

William O. Douglas (1898–1980)—U.S. Supreme Court justice from 1939 to 1975

Woody Guthrie (1912–1967)—most famous folksinger of the first half of the 1900s

H. L. Hunt (1889–1974)—multimillionaire oil tycoon

Louis L'Amour (1908–1988)—novelist famous for his books about the West

Art Linkletter (1912–)—television personality

Eric Sevareid (1912–1992)—reporter and television journalist

matter what their previous jobs had been—sold apples for a nickel apiece on street corners. Throughout the country, people were doing whatever they could to get by—from taking in laundry, to sewing, to scrubbing floors.

Nonprofessional workers, or those with factory or mechanical skills, left their homes and families in hopes of finding work elsewhere. Yet with a nationwide crisis, they frequently remained unemployed. Some of these people became the hobos who "rode the rails" during the Great Depression. With no money for transportation, they would jump into open **boxcars** on freight trains to hitch a ride to their next stop where they would once again look for work.

Hobos atop the cars of a freight train

During the Great Depression, it is estimated that more than 2 million men and eight thousand women rode the rails. But hitching these rides could be risky. The railroad companies hired brutal guards who were known to beat up these rail riders. And jumping onto moving trains could be dangerous. This led to many accidents. Some historians believe more than fifty thousand people were either injured or killed jumping trains.

At times, rail riders would find work for a few weeks picking food crops. But their earnings were never steady or

The strains of unemployment and homelessness took their toll on many Americans who found themselves without any means of support.

enough to make a living. When asked what could be done about so many people wandering throughout America, one social worker replied, "If I had to make such an answer, it would be jobs. Just that. Honest-to-goodness jobs that would let a fellow feel that he's a man, running his own life."

OUT OF THE DUST BOWL

The rail riders were not the only ones on the move during the Great Depression. Many farmers from the southern portion of

* * * *

Even outside of the dustbowl, extreme drought plagued many of the nation's farming communities.

the Great Plains also packed up and left their homes. They had been facing poor economic conditions, drought, and dust storms that made it impossible to grow crops.

One of the reasons the region turned into a dust bowl was poor farming practices. At the time, many farmers did not follow the techniques that would have allowed the earth to hold its moisture. Instead, large numbers of farmers continuously planted more crops, draining the soil of its moisture and the **nutrients** required to grow crops. Over time, the once-fertile soil became dry. When a natural period of drought occurred,

SEEING THE DUST FLY

Lawrence Svobida was a Kansas farmer during the Great Depression.

In his memoirs, he described a dust storm:

> Sometimes [the dust] was so thick that it completely hid the sun. As [the dust storm cloud] sweeps onward, the landscape is progressively blotted out. Birds fly in terror before the storm, and only those that are strong of wing may escape. The smaller birds fly until they are exhausted, then fall to the ground, to share the fate of the thousands of jack rabbits which perish from suffocation.

13

★ ★ ★ ★

The combination of poor farming practices and severe drought resulted in soil erosion, devastating farmland across the country.

the rich layer of **topsoil** dried up and was blown away in the dust storms. In 1935 alone, 850 million tons of topsoil were carried off by the wind. It darkened the sky, causing what became known as "black blizzards."

A black blizzard, or dust storm, rolls across the plains of southeastern Colorado in April 1935.

Now these farm families had to leave the area. They loaded as many belongings as they could onto their cars or pickup trucks and headed west. They were determined to make their way to California from Oklahoma, Arkansas, Kansas, Texas, New Mexico, and Colorado. Some headed to California because they had family members there. Others had seen advertisements showing California as a place with a great climate and available jobs in the agriculture industry.

As poverty-stricken families travelled in search of work, migrant camps became the homes of many.

At times, nearly seven thousand **migrants** a month went west, hoping to find work picking crops. The famous American novelist, John Steinbeck, described their journey in his 1939 book, *The Grapes of Wrath*: "And then the [poor] were drawn west. . . . Carloads, caravans, homeless, and hungry . . . They streamed over mountains hungry and restless—restless as ants, scurrying to find work to do."

But often these Okies, as the press insultingly nicknamed them, were disappointed. So many people wanted work that large numbers were turned away. In 1936 alone, the Los Angeles police force posted more than one hundred extra deputies along California's state line to turn away migrants with no money. The large pool of incoming workers also drove down wages sharply. People weren't able to earn enough money to support their families. Unable to afford adequate housing, many of these migrant workers set up outdoor camps. Sanitation, or clean conditions that prevent disease, became a problem in these camps, and people often became seriously ill.

HOME SWEET HOME

Some Americans' biggest challenge during the Great Depression was keeping a roof over their families' heads. Many who could no longer pay their **mortgages** lost their homes. Apartment dwellers who could not pay their rent were evicted, or thrown out. Some unemployed people were able to keep their homes only by taking in boarders, or people who paid to rent a bedroom in the home. At times, a family had one or more other families living with them. It was crowded, but there weren't a lot of other choices.

In some cases, living conditions were even worse. During the Great Depression, hundreds of Americans lived in poorly constructed shacks or huts in areas known as shantytowns. These shantytowns sprang up in different parts of

After losing their jobs and homes, many people built shacks out of whatever materials they could find.

the country—often in abandoned shipyards or industrial parks. Most shantytown residents were homeless men, although women and children were found there as well. Some shantytowns had as many as one thousand people.

These primitive communities were sometimes called Hoovervilles. They were named for President Herbert Hoover, who served from 1929 to 1933. Many Americans saw him as responsible for the sorry state of their country.

In some cases, entire families found themselves trying to get by as part of a makeshift community in one of the country's many shantytowns.

Elected in a time of prosperity, President Hoover was slow to acknowledge the country's dire economic situation.

HERBERT HOOVER

Things were very different when Herbert Hoover was elected president in 1928. The nation's mood had been upbeat and confident. In accepting his party's presidential nomination, Hoover had said, "We in America today are nearer to the final triumph over poverty than ever before in the history of the land. The poorhouse is vanishing from among us."

Herbert Hoover had been a firm believer in big business. Even after the stock market crash, he failed to realize just how serious the problem was. In November 1929, he told

President Hoover gives a speech in Philadelphia, Pennsylvania, in 1932. After the stock market crash, Hoover was an unpopular president.

the nation: "Any lack of confidence in the economic future or the basic strength of business in the United States is foolish." Even by the spring of the following year, when

Despite President Hoover's promises of improvement, the lines of people in need of food proved that the country's economic depression still remained.

things had gotten considerably worse, Hoover continued to be optimistic. He promised Americans that "the worst effects of the crash upon unemployment will have passed during the next sixty days."

While that was not the case, President Hoover did not believe that government action was needed. Economic difficulties were seen as a natural part of doing business. Hoover believed that the problem would correct itself and that American workers would soon enjoy all the benefits of a full business recovery. But as it turned out, there was no quick recovery, and large numbers of workers continued to lose their jobs.

As time passed, the pressure on Hoover to do something increased. He urged businesses not to get rid of any more workers. But as profits continued to drop, more people were let go. Thinking that a balanced federal budget would restore the nation's confidence and allow businesses to boom again, Hoover finally took action. He ended tax cuts and, at the same time, decreased government spending. This proved to be one of the worst steps he could have taken. It further lessened the amount of money available for purchases, and the economy continued its downward slide.

In 1932, Hoover established the Reconstruction Finance Corporation. The purpose was to provide government funds to banks to allow them to offer more loans to people. Yet few loans were made to those who needed them most, and some

DESPERATE TIMES, DESPERATE MEASURES

During the Great Depression, starving people sometimes took desperate steps. Previously law-abiding citizens stole food for themselves and their children. In some cases, food riots broke out and the police had to be called in. That's what happened in February 1931 in Minneapolis, Minnesota, when a mob broke a grocery store's window and stole meats, fruits, and canned goods. One hundred police were needed to bring the mob under control.

As the economy continued to struggle, many groups demanded government action. One such group was made up of World War I veterans, who demanded payment of their bonuses for their wartime service.

Welthy Americans and religious charities handed out bread and canned food to those who needed it.

said that Hoover's action was more helpful to the banks than to unemployed workers.

Faced with a desperate nation, President Hoover encouraged private charities to help. He claimed that "mutual help through voluntary giving" was the answer. The wealthy responded to his call, and donations poured in. But most charities were overwhelmed by all the help that was needed throughout the country. There simply weren't enough charities, or funds, to help the vast numbers of Americans who remained down and out.

Meanwhile, various citizens' organizations demanded that the government provide some relief for them. One such group consisted of the World War I **veterans** who were supposed to receive cash bonuses for their wartime service. Legislation passed in 1924 promised every serviceman $1.00 for each day served in the United States and $1.25 for each day served overseas. The veterans were not supposed to be paid until 1945, however.

In January 1931, a Texas congressman named Wright Patman introduced legislation that called for the immediate payment of these bonuses. He believed the veterans should be paid in their time of need, not in the distant future. However, President Hoover opposed this measure, arguing that it would further hurt the economy, as well as cost the U.S. government too much. Hoover tried to persuade Congress not to vote for Patman's bill.

Many World War I veterans who had been hit hard by the Great Depression were furious. Calling themselves the Bonus Army, they decided to go to Washington, D.C., to make their voices heard. Many arrived in trucks with slogans painted on them. To remind people of their service in France during World War I, one slogan read, "We did a good job in France. Now, you do a good job in America."

By June 1932, thousands of veterans gathered in the nation's capital to demand what was rightfully theirs. Some had traveled from as far away as Washington State. They set up camps near the White House and the Capitol. The legislation authorizing their immediate payment was voted on in Congress while the veterans were there. Though the bill passed in the House of Representatives, it was defeated in the Senate.

Police in Washington, D.C., try to hold back a crowd of fifteen thousand World War I veterans who are demanding full payment of their war bonuses.

The angry and disappointed veterans refused to leave Washington, D.C., without their money. President Hoover gave them until July 24 to go home. On that day, when they were still there, the police, accompanied by federal troops,

A REVEALING LETTER

Herbert Hoover was firmly against bonus payments for World War I veterans. In a letter dated February 18, 1931, to Senator Reed Smoot, the president explained:

I have supported, and the nation should main-tain, the important principle that when men have been called into jeopardy of their very lives in protection of the Nation, then the Nation as a whole incurs a special obligation beyond that to any other groups of its citizens. These obligations cannot wholly be met with dollars and cents. . . . The country should not be called upon . . . either directly or indirectly, to support or make loans to those who can by their own efforts support themselves. . . . By far the largest part of the huge sum proposed in this bill is to be available to those [veterans] who are not in distress. . . . Such action may quite well result in a [continuation] of this period of unemployment and suffering in which veterans will themselves suffer with others.

tried to remove them by force. Violence broke out, and two veterans were killed. Many Americans were upset by this event, and President Hoover's popularity dipped even further.

A NEW DAY DAWNS

No one was shocked when President Herbert Hoover lost his bid for reelection in 1932. In a landslide victory, the challenger, Franklin D. Roosevelt, became the thirty-second president of the United States. Throughout Roosevelt's 1932 presidential campaign, his views had differed sharply from those of Hoover.

Even President Hoover described the differences between himself and Roosevelt: "This presidential campaign is more than a contest between two men. It is more than a contest between two parties. It is a contest between two [views] of government."

Roosevelt believed that government should take an active role in helping the nation recover. Stressing that he wasn't afraid to try something new, Roosevelt promised "a new deal for the American people" if elected. Roosevelt's New Deal would encompass a variety of programs designed to assist individuals, businesses, and banks.

Though President Roosevelt came from a wealthy family, his parents had taught him the

Franklin D. Roosevelt greets supporters in Washington, D.C., during the final days of his presidential campaign.

importance of taking care of those in need. In his March 4, 1933, inaugural address, Roosevelt assured the American people that brighter days were ahead:

"Our greatest primary task is to put people to work. This is no unsolvable problem if we face it wisely and courageously. It can be accomplished [through] greatly needed projects to stimulate and reorganize the use of our natural

The head of the U.S. Post Office holds signs in support of the National Recovery Act, or the New Deal. Americans who saw these signs were reminded that better days were on the way.

resources. . . . The people of the United States have not failed. In their need . . . they want direct, vigorous action."

Roosevelt wasted no time taking action. In his first one hundred days in office, he worked with Congress to pass fifteen laws to begin his New Deal agencies and programs.

President Roosevelt signs the Emergency Banking Bill, which put him in charge of the country's finances.

In June 1933, the Federal Deposit Insurance Corporation (FDIC) was created by Congress. Through it, the government insured bank deposits for up to $5,000. This meant that even if a bank failed, anyone who had as much as $5,000 deposited in that bank would not lose the money.

FIRESIDE CHATS

On Sunday evening, March 12, 1933, President Roosevelt gave the first of thirty radio addresses that were less formal than his speeches. The addresses were known as Fireside Chats. These chats weren't very long. They ranged in length from fifteen to forty-five minutes. The president used this airtime to explain his New Deal programs and convince Americans that better times were ahead. Roosevelt connected to the public as he warmly invited all Americans to "tell me your troubles." These chats came to mean a great deal to many people throughout the country, who felt that at last they had a president who cared about them. One man described their effect on him: "I never saw [the president], but I knew him."

This helped restore Americans' confidence in the banking system.

Making banking more dependable was just the start of Roosevelt's plan for the nation's recovery. In the months ahead, he would begin a series of other programs. He was determined "to take a method and try it. If it fails, admit it frankly and try another. But above all, try something."

That's precisely what Roosevelt did in April 1933, when he began the Civilian Conservation Corps (CCC). This was a combined relief and employment program especially designed for single men between the ages of seventeen and twenty-seven. The young men signed up for nine-month periods of service and were put to work improving the country's natural landscape. They maintained forests, parks, and beaches, taking pride in doing work that beautified the nation.

In 1936, as the program reached its height, there were more than five hundred thousand participants in the CCC. They were paid only a dollar a day, but they were given a place to live and food. Some also received valuable job training and experience in the area of conservation. Following the success of the CCC, a number of similar programs were started for single women.

* * * *

In August 1933, just months after starting the CCC, President Roosevelt had the government establish the Soil Erosion Service. The idea behind this service was to put unemployed people to work, as well as to restore the areas damaged by drought and dust storms. In many ways, Roosevelt was ahead of his time in his concern for the environment. As he once told the country, "A nation that destroys its soil, destroys itself. Forests are the lungs of our land, purifying the air and giving fresh strength to our people."

Young men in need of work were assigned to the CCC, which provided relief for the unemployed while improving the nation's landscape.

THE TENNESSEE VALLEY AUTHORITY

Among the other agencies Roosevelt started was the Tennessee Valley Authority (TVA). On May 18, 1933, Congress passed the TVA Act. The idea behind it was to bring new life to the Tennessee Valley, an area extending beyond Tennessee into the surrounding states that was especially hard hit by the Great Depression.

Through the TVA, farmers were shown how to increase the amount of crops they harvested. Fertilizers were also produced and sold. Because the area's best timber had already been cut, residents were given help in both replanting forests and learning to control forest fires. Fish and wildlife habitats were also improved.

The most vital change, however, came from having electricity. The TVA built dams to generate electricity, making people's lives easier and more productive. The availability of electricity also brought industry to the Tennessee Valley. As a result, many much-needed jobs were created.

THE WORKS PROGRESS ADMINISTRATION

In April 1935, one of Roosevelt's best-known projects was set in motion. This program, which produced work for nearly 9 million Americans during the depression, was the Works Progress Administration (WPA). (Its name was later changed to the Work Projects Administration.) The WPA helped reduce unemployment as people across the country

An electric power station in Memphis, Tennessee, built by the TVA

were put to work constructing and repairing roads, dams, airports, hospitals, schools, and other public buildings.

Artists, sculptors, musicians, writers, and actors also benefited from the WPA. There were government-spon-

Georgia Flournoy was interviewed for the *American
Slave Narratives* project.

sored concerts and theater productions. Artists were paid
to paint colorful murals, or large paintings, on government
buildings as well.

* * * *

Writers were also kept busy. One especially valuable WPA project they undertook was compiling the *American Slave Narratives*. In doing this, writers interviewed more than 2,300 former slaves. Many of these individuals were quite old, and it was important to capture their life stories before they died. As a result of this project, there exists a firsthand account of what slavery was like in the United States.

OTHER PROGRAMS

Roosevelt's New Deal contained numerous other programs. On August 14, 1935, the Social Security Act was passed to provide an income for older Americans, aid to the disabled, financial assistance for the unemployed, and additional benefits for other groups. The Securities Act of 1933 created the Securities Exchange Commission (SEC), which oversees practices on the New York Stock Exchange. The commission strives to prevent dishonest dealings and to make the stock exchange safe for people who want to invest their money.

Not all of Roosevelt's New Deal programs were successful. Critics called the high number of agencies Roosevelt created an "alphabet soup." They were especially critical of the Agricultural Adjustment Administration (AAA). The AAA paid farmers not to raise certain crops and farm animals. The purpose was to reduce the supply and drive up the prices, which would help the farmers.

As instructed by the AAA, many farmers began destroying crops and killing hogs they had intended to

WPA ART

The WPA provided work for more than five thousand artists. Some were already well known in the art community, but had been unable to sell many paintings during the depression. In other cases, the WPA helped to launch the careers of new artists. Some WPA art still exists and is considered an important reminder of that time in the nation's history.

sell. Americans were outraged when they learned that thousands of hogs had been slaughtered and thrown away. People believed it was wrong to waste food when so many Americans were starving. Despite the criticism, the AAA was successful in assisting farmers. Nevertheless, the U.S. Supreme Court later declared this agency—along with some of President Roosevelt's other New Deal measures—unconstitutional, or illegal, and those programs had to end.

LOOKING BACK AT THE NEW DEAL

Though many people think that the New Deal ended the Great Depression, that is not correct. New Deal programs helped numerous Americans get through a difficult period, and unemployment fell in 1937. But it rose sharply in 1938. The end of the Great Depression actually began in December 1941, after Japan bombed the U.S. naval base at Pearl Harbor, Hawaii.

This event marked the United States' entry into World War II (1939–1945) and the start of a wartime economy. The government provided much more money for the war effort than it provided for New Deal programs. Industry got the boost it needed from the demand for planes, ships, ammunition, and military supplies and equipment necessary to fight the war. Before long, the economy was strong again.

However, the New Deal still changed America in some important ways. It altered how Americans thought about their government. The government's role was no longer viewed as largely that of a wartime protector. Now Ameri-

After male factory workers left their work to fight overseas, women took over their jobs. These women are at work in an airplane factory in May 1942.

cans believed that their government should ensure a good economy as well as look after the health and welfare of its citizens. Today, some New Deal agencies, such as the Social Security Administration, are considered by some to be crucial to the well-being of America's citizens.

The aircraft industry was called an industrial melting pot during World War II. Men and women of many ethnicities worked together to build fighter planes.

40

Following the New Deal, Americans came to think of their homeland as an essentially fair and compassionate nation. They took pride in how this country treated those in need. As President Roosevelt said, "The test of our progress is not whether we add more to the abundance of those who have much; it is whether we provide enough for those who have too little." It was an important lesson—one that was learned through the Great Depression to current times.

One of the lasting lessons of the Great Depression is Americans should help those in need. This present-day photograph shows a group of teenagers serving food at a soup kitchen.

Glossary

boxcars—enclosed railroad cars with sliding doors on the sides

drought—a long period without rain

economy—the way a country runs its industry, trade, and finance

goods—things that are bought and sold

migrants—people who move often in search of work

mortgages—loans from banks to buy houses

nutrients—the minerals in soil that make it good for growing crops

scavenge—to search among garbage for food

stock—a share, or piece, of a company that people purchase as an investment

stockbrokers—people who arrange the sale and purchase of stocks

stock exchange—a place where trading is conducted based on an organized system

stock market—the money that is available for investment or trading

topsoil—the top or surface level of soil

trading floor—the area in a stock exchange where stockbrokers and investors buy and sell stocks

tycoons—wealthy, powerful businesspeople

veterans—people who have served in the U.S. armed forces

Wall Street—site of the New York Stock Exchange and many of the companies that heavily influence the U.S. economy

Timeline: The Great

1928	1929	1931		1932	1933	
NOVEMBER 6 Herbert Hoover is elected president.	**OCTOBER 29** The stock market crashes on the day known as Black Tuesday.	**FEBRUARY** A mob riots for food in Minneapolis, Minnesota.	**SUMMER** Severe drought hits the southern portion of the Great Plains region.	**NOVEMBER 8** Franklin D. Roosevelt is elected president.	**MARCH 12** President Roosevelt gives his first Fireside Chat.	**APRIL** The Civilian Conservation Corps (CCC) is begun.

Map of the United States showing the Dust Bowl and Extreme drought regions.

CANADA

Washington · Montana · North Dakota · Minnesota · Minneapolis · Wisconsin · Great Lakes · Michigan · Maine

Oregon · Idaho · South Dakota · New York · Vt. · N.H.

Wyoming · Iowa · Pennsylvania · New York City · Mass. · R.I. · Conn. · N.J.

Nevada · UNITED STATES · Nebraska · Ohio · Indiana · Illinois · Washington, D.C. · Del. · Md.

Utah · Colorado · Kansas · Missouri · Kentucky · W. Va. · Virginia · ATLANTIC OCEAN

California · Los Angeles

Arizona · New Mexico · Oklahoma · Arkansas · Tennessee · North Carolina · South Carolina

PACIFIC OCEAN · Texas · Miss. · Alabama · Georgia · Louisiana · Florida

☐ Dust Bowl
▨ Extreme drought

MEXICO · Gulf of Mexico

N

0   200   400
Distance in miles

Depression

MAY 18	JUNE	APRIL	AUGUST 14		DECEMBER 7	DECEMBER 8
Congress authorizes the Tennessee Valley Authority (TVA).	The Federal Deposit Insurance Corporation (FDIC) is created.	The Works Progress Administration (WPA) is started.	President Roosevelt signs the Social Security Act into law.	Unemployment rises despite the New Deal.	Japan bombs the U.S. naval base in Pearl Harbor, Hawaii.	The United States enters World War II. Over the next few years, the wartime economy ends the Great Depression.

To Find Out More

BOOKS

Allport, Alan. *Franklin Delano Roosevelt*. Broomall, Pa.: Chelsea House, 2004.

Brennan, Kristine. *The Stock Market Crash of 1929*. Broomall, Pa.: Chelsea House, 2000.

Coombs, Karen Mueller. *Children of the Dust Days*. Minneapolis: Carolrhoda Books, 2000.

Cooper, Michael L. *Dust to Eat: Drought and Depression in the 1930s*. New York: Clarion Books, 2004.

ONLINE SITES

The Depression & World War II (1929–1945)
http://www.americaslibrary.gov/cgi-bin/page.cgi/jb/wwii

The Dust Bowl
http://www.usd.edu.anth/epa/dust.html

The New Deal
http://www.newdeal.feri.org/index.htm

Photographs of the Great Depression
http://www.history1900s.about.com/library/photos/blyindexdepression.htm

President Franklin D. Roosevelt
http://www.whitehouse.gov/history/presidents/fr32.html

To Find Out More

BOOKS

Allport, Alan. *Franklin Delano Roosevelt*. Broomall, Pa.: Chelsea House, 2004.

Brennan, Kristine. *The Stock Market Crash of 1929*. Broomall, Pa.: Chelsea House, 2000.

Coombs, Karen Mueller. *Children of the Dust Days*. Minneapolis: Carolrhoda Books, 2000.

Cooper, Michael L. *Dust to Eat: Drought and Depression in the 1930s*. New York: Clarion Books, 2004.

ONLINE SITES

The Depression & World War II (1929–1945)
http://www.americaslibrary.gov/cgi-bin/page.cgi/jb/wwii

The Dust Bowl
http://www.usd.edu.anth/epa/dust.html

The New Deal
http://www.newdeal.feri.org/index.htm

Photographs of the Great Depression
http://www.history1900s.about.com/library/photos/blyindexdepression.htm

President Franklin D. Roosevelt
http://www.whitehouse.gov/history/presidents/fr32.html

Depression

MAY 18	JUNE	APRIL	AUGUST 14	Unemployment	DECEMBER 7	DECEMBER 8
Congress authorizes the Tennessee Valley Authority (TVA).	The Federal Deposit Insurance Corporation (FDIC) is created.	The Works Progress Administration (WPA) is started.	President Roosevelt signs the Social Security Act into law.	ment rises despite the New Deal.	Japan bombs the U.S. naval base in Pearl Harbor, Hawaii.	The United States enters World War II. Over the next few years, the wartime economy ends the Great Depression.

Index

Bold numbers indicate illustrations.

About the Author

Award-winning author **Elaine Landau** received a bachelor's degree in English and journalism from New York University and a master's degree in library and information science from Pratt Institute. She worked as a newspaper reporter, a children's book editor, and a youth services librarian before becoming a full-time writer. She has written more than two hundred nonfiction books for children and young adults. She lives in Miami, Florida, with her husband, Norman, and their son, Michael.